CLAUDE AKE MEMORIAL PAPER

A (Wo)man for all seasons:
AMOS TUTUOLA AND THE GENDERING OF PEACE IN AFRICA

By Heidi Hudson

Claude Ake Visiting Chair 2018 at
the Nordic Africa Institute and Uppsala University

Professor of international relations and director of the
Centre of African Studies at the University of Free State,
Bloemfontein, South Africa

NORDISKA AFRIKAINSITUTET OCH UPPSALA UNIVERSITET
The Nordic Africa Institute and Uppsala University

UPPSALA 2019

INDEXING TERMS:

Amos Tutuola
Literature
Feminism
Women
Peacebuilding
Gender analysis
Folklore
Criticism

A (Wo)man for all seasons: Amos Tutuola and the Gendering of Peace in Africa
Claude Ake Memorial Paper No. 11
By Heidi Hudson

ISBN 978-91-7106-839-2   print-on-demand version
ISBN 978-91-7106-840-8   pdf e-book
ISBN 978-91-7106-841-5   epub e-book
ISSN 1654-7489

© 2019 The author and the Nordic Africa Institute

Layout and production editor: Henrik Alfredsson, the Nordic Africa Institute
Language editor: James Middleton
Print on demand: Lightning Source UK Ltd.

Front cover: El Fasher, North Darfur, September 2013. Women celebrating the UN International Day of Peace. Photo: Albert González Farran, Unamid.

THE NORDIC AFRICA INSTITUTE (Nordiska Afrikainstitutet) is a centre for research, knowledge, policy advice and information on Africa. Based in Uppsala, Sweden, we are a government agency, funded jointly by Sweden, Finland and Iceland.

The opinions expressed in this volume are those of the author and do not necessarily reflect the views of the Nordic Africa Institute.

This work is made available under a Creative Commons Attribution-Non Commercial-No Derivatives 4.0 International (CC BY-NC-ND 4.0) Licence. Details regarding permitted usage can be found at WWW.CREATIVECOMMONS.ORG/LICENSES/BY-NC-ND/4.0

This work is freely available in open access, you can download it online via the NAI web site, www.nai.uu.se, where you can also purchase print edition copies.

Contents

Foreword 5

Abstract 7

Preface and acknowledgements 9

Introduction 11

The decolonisation imperative – peacebuilding and gender challenges 17

The Complete Gentleman, agency and the feminist intersecionality project 25

Shifting political identities: Big Men as complete gentlemen? 32

Making the everyday spectral, spectacular and uncomfortable 37

From othering to liminality: implications for gender and peacebuilding 45

Conclusion 51

Bibliography 52

About the Claude Ake Visiting Chair and Memorial Paper 56

Foreword

On November 7, 1996 the internationally respected social scientist Claude Ake died at the age of 57 in a plane crash outside Lagos, Nigeria. He was well known as one of Africa's leading researchers in political economy and development affairs. He was a proponent of democracy and social justice in Africa. He was a frequent visitor to Uppsala University, Sweden, particularly the Department of Peace and Conflict Research, and to the Nordic Africa Institute. To honor his legacy, the University and the Nordic Africa Institute created the Claude Ake Visiting Chair in 2003. For 15 years this chair has given the opportunity for African researchers at African universities to get a semester off in order to further their own studies, and at the same time, help to bring recent social science research in and on Africa to audiences in the Nordic countries. In 2016, a 20-Year Memorial Day on the legacy of Clause Ake was organized in Uppsala by the programme.

In the book *Democracy and Development in Africa*, published in the same year as he died, Ake demonstrated that autocratic governance is the central problem for Africa, and the explanation for why three decades of independence had not yet resulted in a thriving African economy and a lifting of people out of poverty: "By all indications, political conditions in Africa are the greatest impediment to development". This is turn resulted from the particular experience of colonialism in Africa which was build around the "colonial state", which was inherited at the time of independence. Thus, he not only questioned the economic wisdom of the time with its emphasis on stabilization, but also saw a need for political regimes beyond one-party states and military rulers. This perspective led him to criticize widespread state corruption, not least witnessed in his own country.

As for this Claude Ake Memorial Paper by Professor Heidi Hudson, Claude Ake Visiting Chair 2018, there are many intersections between the authorships of the academic scholar Claude Ake (1939-1996) and the folklore novelist Amos Tutuola (1920-1997). Although a generation apart, they were both fervent anti-colonialists and inspiring voices in a time that saw the shaping of an independent Nigeria, the rending effects of civil war and the human rights abuses of a corrupt military regime.

Claude Ake and Amos Tutuola both died in the mid-1990's. None of them lived to see the transition to democracy that country has witnessed in the past two decades. Still, this experience confirms some of Ake's basic ideas of the need for an open society for economic and social development, as well as for academic freedom.

Uppsala, Sweden, 12 December 2018

Peter Wallensteen
Senior Professor, Peace and Conflict Research, Uppsala University, Nordic Africa Institute Associate and Member of the Founding Committee of the Claude Ake Visiting Chair.

Amos Tutuola (1920-1997)

Illustration: Henrik Alfredsson, the Nordic Africa Institute.

Abstract

This book explores the work of Nigerian author Amos Tutuola and how it can enhance our understanding of gender and peacebuilding in Africa. Critical feminist contributions on how a gender perspective can broaden inclusion in post-conflict processes, as well as change institutions and mindsets are surely innovative but have not succeeded in dislodging liberal peace as the means of dealing with conflict on the African continent. Such works also draw their critiques from largely rationalist, Western roots.

While Tutuola's universe shares many assumptions with feminist thinking on peace and security (such as fluidity, complexity and multiplicity), he offers an epistemological extension. His work extends feminist debates about human agency and relational thinking to include the spiritual world of consciousness. Thus, he reminds us to shed our Western rationalities and think and act with daring imagination, looking and seeing beyond the obvious. He skilfully disrupts hierarchical thinking by allowing his characters multiple, temporary forms and hybrid identities that cross over into a non-human world.

Entering Tutuola's world, where human and non-human characters change and interchange, allows scholars and practitioners to see peacebuilding as organic, reliant on multiple identities and interlocutors, and grounded in local knowledge. I contend that such an expanded lens that integrates exogenous and endogenous knowledge systems non-hierarchically is not only relevant to the peacebuilding context, but could also find application in other areas in need of decolonisation.

Key words: *Tutuola, gender, peacebuilding, intersectionality, everyday, Africa, interlocutor*

Uppsala University Main Building

Preface and acknowledgements

I have been humbled by the occasion to come to Uppsala for three months of concentrated research and vivid exchange with the network of colleagues at the Department of Peace and Conflict Research, Uppsala University, and the Nordic Africa Institute. I present the results of my research in this memorial paper, which is based on a lecture that I gave in Uppsala on 21 November 2018, in honour of Prof. Claude Ake, the renowned social sciences scholar-activist. I wish to take the opportunity to thank my hosts in Uppsala, namely: Ms Iina Soiri, director of the Nordic Africa Institute; Prof. Erik Melander, head of the Department of Peace and Conflict Research; Prof. Anders Themnér, chair of the Claude Ake Selection Committee; and Ms Annika Franklin, for making my stay such a memorable one.

Uppsala, Sweden, 22 November 2018

Heidi Hudson
Claude Ake Visiting Chair 2018

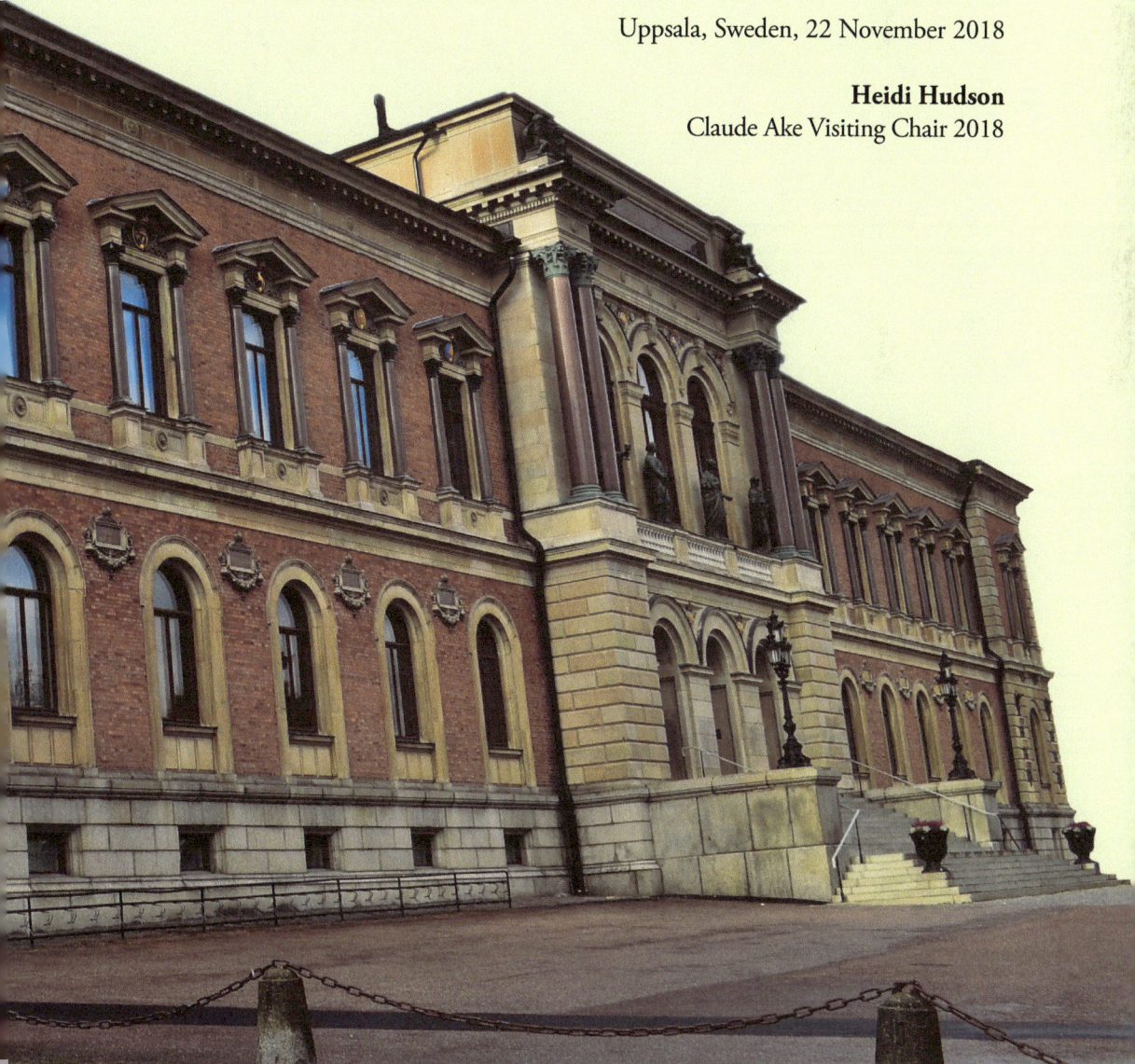

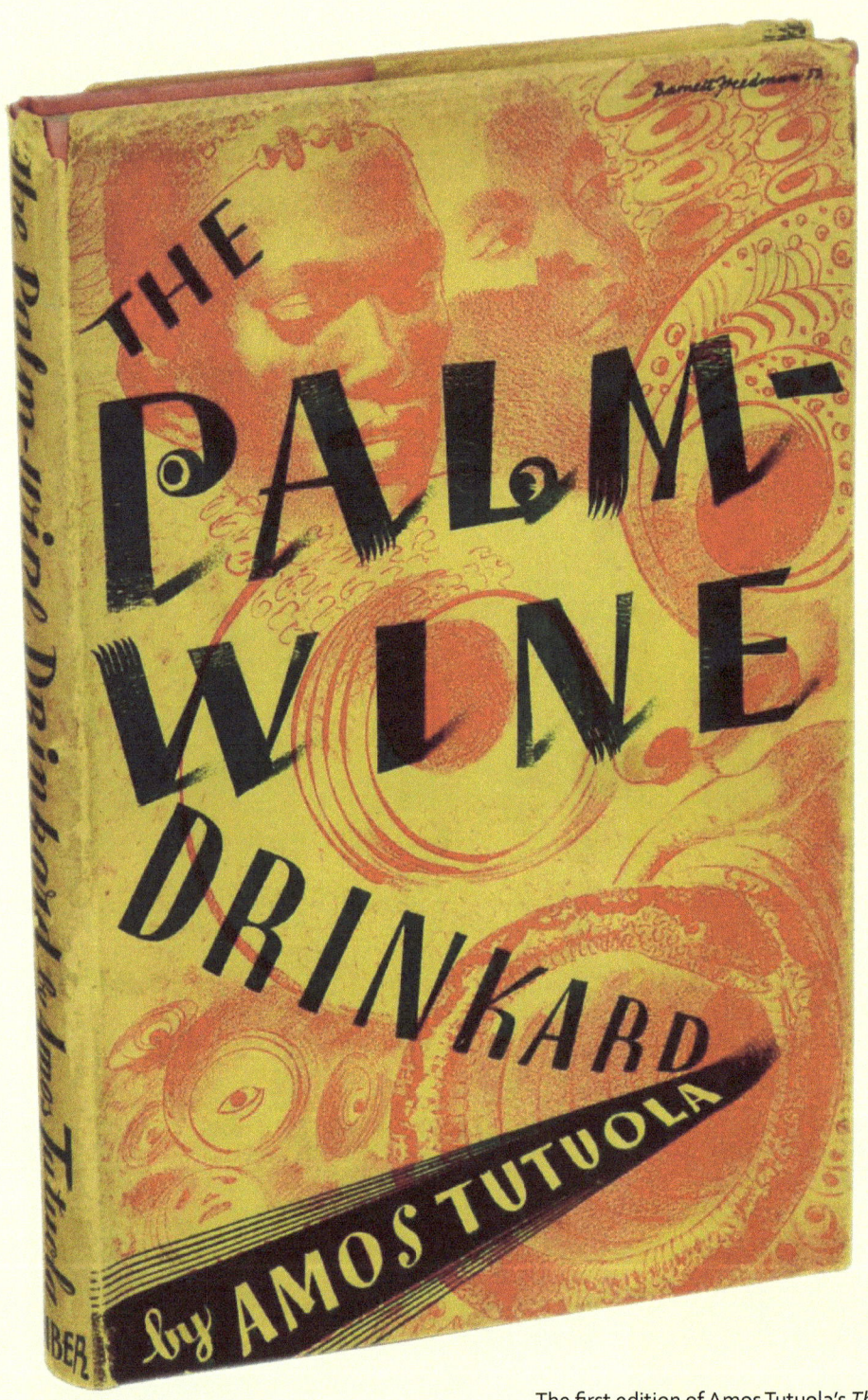

The first edition of Amos Tutuola's *The Palm-Wine Drinkard*, published in 1952 by the UK publihing house Faber & Faber.

Introduction

Let me begin with a few disclaimers. Firstly, I will be addressing you as a scholar of feminist international relations (IR) committed to the need to practise one's discipline – or interdiscipline – in context; I'm not an African literature specialist. Secondly, time does not permit me to go into detail about the similarities between Claude Ake and Amos Tutuola. Suffice it to say that they shared a revolutionary eclecticism that foregrounded fundamental questions about inclusion and exclusion ('who counts as human, who counts as African'), African agency, and a commitment to change on the ground. Reading Ake and Tutuola together offers us a rich repository to draw on for the decolonisation of knowledge project (see, e.g. Arowosegbe, 2012). Lastly, I am not going to provide you with a ready-made toolkit or recipe for applying Tutuola to gender and peacebuilding, but I will outline a specific lens and illustrate it by means of a few examples from the gender and peacebuilding world in Africa.

Amos Tutuola (born in 1920, in Abeokuta, Nigeria; died in 1997) only had six years of formal schooling. He worked as a metalworker and blacksmith, was a messenger for the labour department in Lagos, and also served in the British Royal Air Force (1943-1945). His first full-length book, *The Palm-Wine Drinkard and his Dead Palm-Wine Tapster in the Deads' Town*, written in 1946, was first published in 1952. His second book, *My Life in the Bush of Ghosts*, appeared in 1954. Of all his books, *Simbi and the Satyr of the Dark Jungle* (1955) – the story of a beautiful and rich young girl who leaves her home and experiences poverty and starvation – has the strongest gender theme. I nevertheless chose to focus on The Palm-Wine Drinkard because this is his most widely known work, and is also a much "more complex and subversive book than it has generally been given credit for being" (Tobias, 1999, p. 66). This also explains the choice of title for this paper, 'A (Wo)man for All Seasons': staying true to challenging dominant Eurocentric metanarratives of completeness and autonomy (Nyamnjoh, 2017, p. 112), but doing it through an art of plasticity with creatures that are able to adapt to all circumstances and times.

For the purposes of this paper, I do not concern myself with the politics surrounding the origin of Tutuola's creative ideas – which echo D. O. Fagunwa, his predecessor, who writes in Yoruba – nor the controversy surrounding the reception of the work. The Palm-Wine Drinkard received huge accolades in the UK and the US, but was severely criticised in Tutuola's native Nigeria, because his so-called 'uneducated' and primitive style of using the English language ostensibly reinforced stereotypes of African backwardness. Today his unconventional use of the English language is interpreted as an expression of challenging the empire, and a way of resisting colonial rule. Tutuola's work defies categorisation, and to label him as either a traditionalist, a modernist or a postmodernist simply is not productive for what I want to convey. He mixes Christian and Western elements with Yoruba folklore, marked by a mythical, supernatural world imbued with a peculiar sense of horror as a source of humour. The end 'product' is a hybrid concoction that makes both sophisticated African writers and Western writers who are culturally incapable of such writing profoundly uncomfortable (VanderMeer, 2013).

Therefore, it suits me to think of The Palm-Wine Drinkard as a folktale, where anything is possible and all time and space are suspended, and I can then ask you as the audience to adopt an ambivalent and open reading with me. Literature serves a double function; namely, to reflect the preoccupations of society, but also to challenge them (Edkins, 2013, p. 282). Similar to when one narrates women's stories, storytelling has practical effect: it demands specificity and concreteness, and not just telling one story but many overlapping ones. This not only works against the erection of binaries, but also offers the reader the possibility to judge the stories politically. So, I'm asking you to consider the political relevance of The Palm-Wine Drinkard to the field of gender and peacebuilding. Lately, we have seen a steady revival of Tutuola, but so far not yet in the context of peace and conflict.

> I was a palm-wine drinkard since I was a boy of ten years of age. I had no other work more than to drink palm-wine in my life. (Tutuola, 1952, p. 7)

These opening lines of the book introduce the reader to the story of a lazy rich boy whose palm-wine tapster provides him with an endless supply of palm-wine, until one day when the tapster is killed. And with that the narrator's, i.e. the drinkard's, supply of palm-wine abruptly dries up and he finds himself without drinking buddies. He then embarks on a journey to Deads' Town to find his tapster, coming into contact with many non-human creatures and having many narrow escapes. In Deads' Town, he receives a gift of a magic egg from his dead tapster, enabling him to produce anything he wants from the egg. Eventually the drinkard returns home and settles a dispute between the Sky God and the Earth Goddess, thereby putting an end to a drought that the Sky God caused to spite the earth (Obiechina, 1968, pp. 87-88).

In the first part of the presentation, I make a case for nuanced and multiple approaches to decolonisation and highlight the limited transformation that has taken place in the field of peacebuilding and gender. In the next two sections, I look at how Tutuola extends the feminist work on overcoming binaries and refer specifically to his contribution to the concept of intersectionality and agency, and how he has added a spiritual dimension to the study of the everyday. In the final section, I look at the character of the drinkard as a 'go-between' and explore the relevance of this notion for challenging liberal peacebuilding and the liberal mainstreaming of gender from an Afrocentric perspective.

Ife, Nigeria. Obatala priests in their temple. Photo: Dierk Lange, 2000.

In Yoruba lore, Obatala is an *orisha*, an incarnated spirit, who was brought to life by the supreme deity Olodumare and descended from the heavens on a golden chain to create the earth and the humans. But on his mission, Obatala found palm wine which he drank and became intoxicated.

> The character of the drinkard is such a kind of marvellous mutant-mediator of different physical and meta-physical worlds.

Professor Francis Nyamnjoh during his keynote speech at the Nordic Africa Days in Uppsala, Sweden, September 2018.

The decolonisation imperative – peacebuilding and gender challenges

So, what does African folklore have to do with gender and peacebuilding in Africa? Building on the work of Nyamnjoh (2015a; 2015b; 2017), who suggested to me to consider the gender theme in Tutuola's work, my so-called 'literary turn' was motivated by a deep-seated disenchantment with IR as a largely state-centric enterprise, as well as the lack of progress made by feminist IR scholars to dismantle these vestiges of power, specifically in the area of peacebuilding on the continent. All this happened against the backdrop of the Rhodes Must Fall and Fees Must Fall movements in South Africa, which have attracted global attention, but which also contain within them, I believe, the seeds of recolonisation.

In the month before I came to Uppsala, I attended a conference on decolonisation at the University of Johannesburg. In his welcome speech, Vice Chancellor Prof. Tshilidzi Marwala stated that is much easier to transform demographics rather than tackling the shift from superstitious to scientific thinking. He emphasised that it does not mean moving away from culture, but rather that Africa must move into the era of the Fourth Industrial Revolution. If Africa is left behind, the continent becomes a spectator, not a participant in the future system where human beings and machines will merge into one.

Plausible as it may seem on one level, I think assumptions about the binary between science and superstition are quite precarious. They underline the reality that African elites have also bought into the Eurocentric dismissal of "such consciousness as magic, witchcraft, primitivism and superstition" (Nyamnjoh, 2015a, p. 3). And this explains why Tutuola's Yoruba folktales have remained unrecognised until recently, even in Nigeria. Education kills superstition – or rather, attention to the spiritual – and, more importantly, the ability to imagine alternative futures, and replaces it with a rational practical mind (VanderMeer, 2013). This kind of thinking feeds into the coloniality of knowledge, treating the knowledge of the ordinary or the knowledge of those we do not understand as traditional and hence inferior.

The current debates on decolonisation, in South Africa, in particular, are quite one-sided and narrowly prescriptive in how to go about it. The dominant radical version hinges on a very stark coloniser/colonised binary. But let's not pretend there is only one way to decolonise. For Long (2016) the term "imprisons us within a colonial imaginary. Unable to think beyond…white and black, stripped of the potential for audacious acts of imagination". Reinforcing old binaries could run the risk of recolonisation and inscribing what you set out to criticise (Keet 2018). The more we deconstruct the coloniality of Europe, the greater the risk of recentring Europe. As Hobson and Sajed (2017) rightly remark:

> If prior to the linguistic turn, we dealt with a sovereign and self-sufficient Western subject, after the linguistic turn we are now witnessing a fragmented and deconstructed Western self, wherein focus continues to lie squarely on the Western subject, albeit in a fashionably mournful and melancholic posture (p. 557)

At the other end of the spectrum, simply inserting Tutuola and his endogenous knowledge into the Western debate is unlikely to transform anything, and would negate the fact that all knowledges are entangled and that we should be critical of all settled knowledge. Moreover, decoloniality is not only an epistemology, but also an ontology. It helps to remember that intellectual transformation with no link to material transformation – changing conditions and not only positions – fundamentally disrespects the realities of colonialism and generations of suffering.

These problems on how to decolonise are mirrored in the thinking and practices of peacebuilding on the continent, as well as in how gender mainstreaming is conducted. Radically digging down to structural, institutional contradictions and root causes to prevent conflict from breaking out again has been difficult to achieve due to the complexity of many of the conflicts. Peacebuilding is largely overshadowed by its much more muscle-bound 'sister' intervention of peacekeeping as a means to contain direct violence. The liberal cultural project of changing attitudes through peacemaking has concentrated on achieving gender equality and the inclusion of women in security institutions and political decision-making, with the assumption that their peaceful nature will help change hypermasculine militarist institutions.

Peacebuilders include a broad swathe of people, both professional and amateur, working in their own countries or as internationals in conflict-prone countries. They include practitioners in the areas of humanitarian aid, economic development, institution- and nation-building, human rights and advocacy, conflict prevention, conflict resolution and reconciliation, as well as environmental conservation and protection. In addition, any educational, social and structural initiative that has as its aim positive social change, the pursuit of root causes and the prevention of recurrence of violence can be classified as peacebuilding (Petra Peacebuilders, 2018). While much good work is happening, the dominant peacebuilding approach is one that privileges stabilisation and institution-building, particularly state-building, in order to improve issues of implementation, coherence, resource allocation and local interaction (Paris & Sisk, 2009). All actions are guided by the responsibility to uphold international norms of human rights, democratic governance and the market economy. Although some superficial attention is paid to bottom-up initiatives, in practice the relationship between state and civil society is reduced to an inter-elite – foreign and domestic – consensus. The emphasis on technical and procedural matters of state-building often leads to a view of democracy as zero-sum (the only rationally accepted and desired project), with a formal and low-intensity peace as the outcome (Bercovitch & Jackson, 2009). Driven by a belief in the superiority of reason over other forms of knowing, peacebuilding is seen as the responsibility of the Western 'Self' because the non-Western 'Other' is either unwilling or unable to maintain peace. Sadly, influential critiques of the liberal peace, by Duffield (2001) among others, have had the unintended consequence of presenting African subjects as passive or absent. And with the liberal peace quick to adopt the language of local ownership and hybrid global-local peace, it is pretty much business as usual.

Since 2000, with the adoption of UN Security Council Resolution 1325 on Women, Peace and Security, the differential impact of conflict on women and men, as well as the important contribution of women to peacebuilding, have been firmly recognised. Some feminists have, however, criticised the language of the resolution, arguing that rights-based discourses of gender equality limit alternative imaginings to think beyond liberal democracy and a free market economy. Feminist norms and women's rights are consequently hijacked to serve international development and security interests (Pratt & Richter-Devroe, 2011). In practice, it also leads to an almost exclusive focus on women. Women become a synonym for gender, which entrenches the separation between men occupying the public space of the protector and women the private space of protected. The feminist imagination is further kept in check when these critiques originate from mainly Western sources, rather than fully appreciating the politics of space (the postcolony) and how the colonial cuts through our understandings of gender (Lugones, 2008, 2010; Mama, 1995).

That said, what we need is not more abstract critique of the liberal peace, but methodologies that are nuanced enough to account for multiple colonial systems of oppression, as well as the ontological life-worlds of real people (Tucker, 2018). While peacebuilding, in theory, is all about transformation, we need to recognise that there are many intractable aspects of post-war society that are very slow to change. And while the feminist tool of intersectionality (to be discussed in the next section) is most of the time viewed as a means of transformation, it also offers us a way of understanding exactly why change is so difficult to achieve. These multiple overlapping identities of an individual are sometimes a source of agency and sometimes not. Context is therefore key to understanding these dynamics.

Tutuola offers us two interlinked 'tools' – storytelling and imagination – to unlock the underworld of The Palm-Wine Drinkard, and the Yoruba life-world where there is no split between the spirit world and the 'real' world (Hart, 2009, p. 181). If we then say that decolonisation is about (re)discovering "deep relational ontologies between humans, and humans and nature" (Rojas, 2016, p. 369), the struggle for social and epistemic justice ceases to be framed around an impossible nature/culture binary. The answer to overcoming binary thinking about liberal selves and illiberal 'Others' in post-conflict situations may therefore lie outside the confines of Western rationality. The character of the drinkard is such a kind of marvellous mutant-mediator of different physical and metaphysical worlds (Omelsky, 2018, p. 89; Hart, 2009, p. 177): human/non-human, public/private, conflict/peace, colonial/postcolonial, outsider/insider, spiritual/material, as well as between different knowledge systems (Western/indigenous or local, theory/practice). He is able to change his physical shape at will, effortlessly moving from human to non-human form, from the lands of the living to those of the dead.

Tutuola's universe shares many assumptions with feminist thinking on peace and security (such as fluidity, complexity and multiplicity), but he offers an epistemological extension. His work importantly extends feminist debates about human agency and relational thinking to include the spiritual world of consciousness. This is what I want to focus on now in the following two sections. Firstly, I focus on how Tutuola extends the feminist understanding of intersectionality, identity and agency (viewed through the story of the complete gentleman); and secondly, what his spiritual dimension contributes to the feminist study of the everyday.

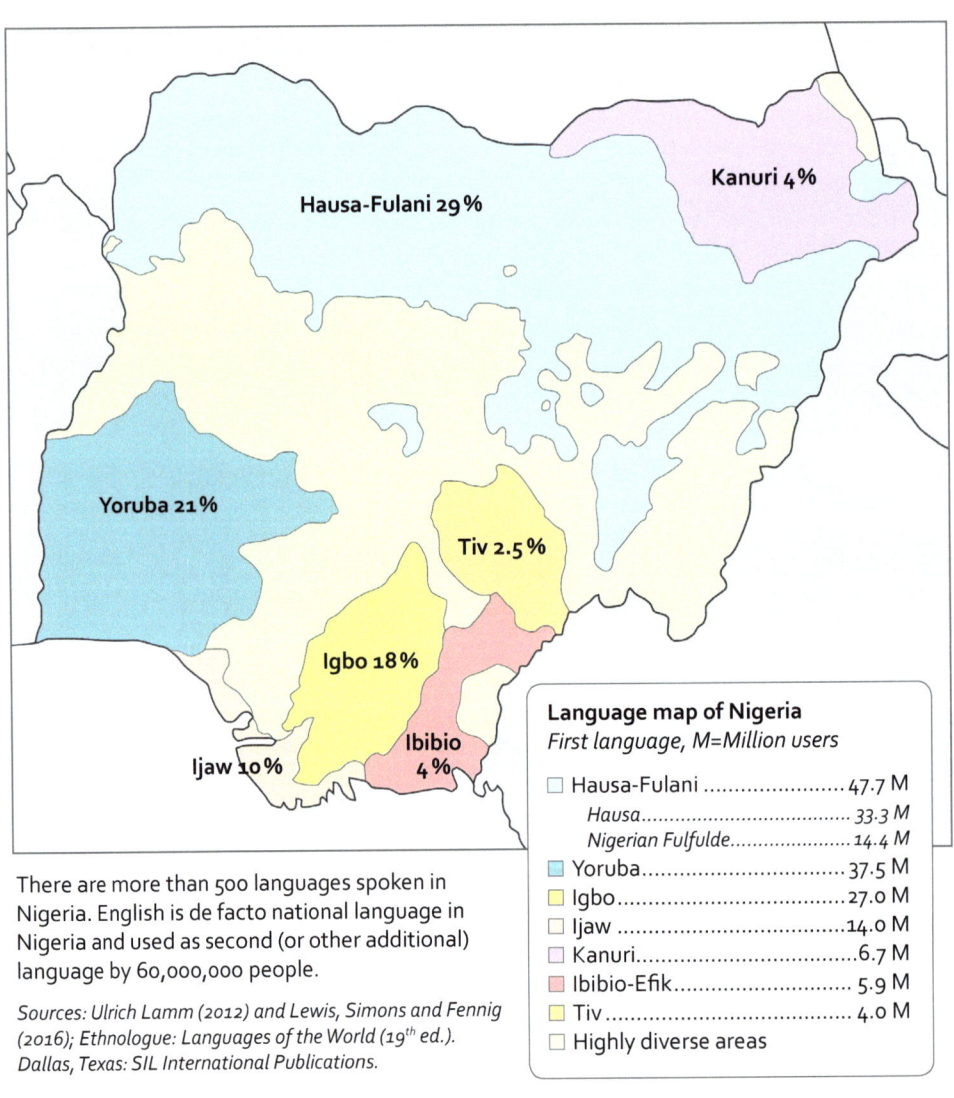

There are more than 500 languages spoken in Nigeria. English is de facto national language in Nigeria and used as second (or other additional) language by 60,000,000 people.

Sources: Ulrich Lamm (2012) and Lewis, Simons and Fennig (2016); Ethnologue: Languages of the World (19th ed.). Dallas, Texas: SIL International Publications.

Women in the conflict-prone North Kivu Province of DR Congo, learning how to bake bread and farm mushrooms in a UN project to promote diversity of livelihood opportunities. Photo: Michael Ali, Monusco, October 2018.

> Changing gender relations have proved to be a source of agency for many women in the Democratic Republic of Congo.

Illustration: Based on Bell telephone magazine 1922

The Complete Gentleman, agency and the feminist intersecionality project

Folktales contain an implicit gender hierarchy, because women usually narrate folktales to children and other women in the evenings; men recount legends – considered to be superior as they are historical or pseudo-historical accounts of events – to other men. Folktales therefore often reflect social roles and expectations (Florence, 2013, p. 371). But I argue that we should read the gender dimension in The Palm-Wine Drinkard, the little that there is, with an open mind and view it in the context of the broader questions that both feminists and Tutuola ask; namely, who belongs, who speaks, who has agency.

It appears as if the 'beautiful lady', later the drinkard's wife (given to him as a reward for rescuing her from the Complete Gentleman), is merely an appendage of the drinkard, indecisive and dependent. This is juxtaposed with the so-called expression of Yoruba manliness through the practice of drinking (Salamone, 2006, p. 203), which we see in the opening line of the book. Read through modern or postmodern eyes, the beautiful lady is the typical female object and gendered 'Other'. We learn that the daughter of the head of the town was a headstrong 'lady', refusing to marry anybody, becoming enthralled by the 'Complete Gentleman' and insisting on following him despite his warnings. But, in the end, she was subdued and had to be saved by the drinkard (Tutuola, 1952, pp. 18-26). The girl's decision to choose the man she wants to marry from outside the community is contrary to the communalist spirit, violating the closed and homogeneous view that the community has of itself, not allowing for multiple identities. But her beauty also makes her valuable to the community in a symbolic sense and she can therefore not be allowed to follow her heart. The girl lacks agency and has to submit to the "normative gender inequality of the community" (Goodhead, 2018, p. 63). And, to make matters worse, her temporary agency is subdued by making her lose her voice, literally, and she becomes a slave (p. 69).

But Tutuola's depiction is not just a simple, one-dimensional, androcentric discourse. The girl becomes the typical "ever-faithful and helpful female companion (typical of heroic myths)" (Moore, 1975, p. 52), far from gender equal, but also not quite fitting the traditional patriarchal conception. Towards the end of the journey, her agency appears to increase, and we actually begin to hear her voice as well. While in the Red-Town, the wife starts speaking in riddles like a foreteller: "This would be a brief loss of woman, but a shorter separation of a man from lover" (Tutuola, 1952, p. 78). In the engagement with the Invisible-Pawn, the drinkard turns to his wife for advice, and she responds, "Wonderful hard worker, but he would be a wonderful robber in future" (pp. 86, 90). In the Wrong-Town, with the Wise-King and the Prince-Killer, his wife predicts the presence of a Wise-King (p. 95) and takes charge when she figures out that people who have not died cannot enter the town by day, and therefore tells the drinkard that they "should stop and rest till night" (p. 95). When hiding and watching while the hero fights the Creatures-in-Bag, she sees how the main creature revives the others and does the same with the drinkard; they are then able to escape (p. 106). Shortly after that he turns his wife into a wooden doll, which could be seen as reverting back to an inferior role, being infantilised and objectified as a wooden toy (p. 108). However, these examples convey the fact that agency is complex and multi-layered.

Turning to the world of conflict and peacebuilding, we see similar manifestations. There is a common assumption that violent masculine subcultures were one of the main causes of the brutal wars in Sierra Leone. Everyday narratives however reveal much more:

> Late one evening, a 10-year-old with a pistol came, alone, into our house. He told my husband his commander was hungry and wanted one of our chickens. While my husband was catching the hen, that boy sat down to wait. He was thin and exhausted. I brought him a biscuit and water. He said he was tired and weak and as he left with the chicken he turned to me and said, 'thank you, mam'. Later my neighbours criticized me for giving him the biscuit. I said I didn't care if he was a rebel or not. He's still somebody's child. (Cockburn, 2007, p. 42)

In this narrative, is it possible for the perpetrator to also be a victim?

The feminist strategy of intersectionality (Crenshaw, 1991), with its focus on multiple intersecting identities, offers a means to counter gender-binary stereotypes of men as protectors and/or aggressors and women as peaceful mothers. This approach has only recently gained traction in peacebuilding practitioner circles in the form of a gender-relational approach to peacebuilding, where the interplay between gender and other identity markers such as age, social class, sexuality, disability, ethnic or religious background, marital status or urban/rural setting is emphasised (Myrttinen et al. 2014). Yet one wonders to what extent it loses its subversive potential when it is just the superficial acknowledgement of difference while upholding whiteness, middle class privilege and heterosexuality as the norm. For the concept to work in practice, it requires intentional engagement with oppression and the need to engage with discomfort.

Tutuola's drinkard hero entertains us with the display of multiple persona and forms, human and non-human faces as trickster, maverick and rogue. He is quick-witted and catches on when the old man asks him to bring back Death, realising that the old man actually wants Death to kill him. At the same time, he also makes us deeply uncomfortable. Many of the creatures we encounter as he journeys to the underworld are cruel and creepy to say the least, such as the red fish, the drinkard's monster child and the hungry-creature.

One such creature is the Complete Gentleman. The beautiful lady falls in love with the Complete Gentleman, described as "a beautiful 'complete' gentleman, he dressed with the finest and most costly clothes, all the parts of his body were completed, he was a tall man but stout" (Tutuola, 1952, p. 18). She follows him into the forest, where he gradually starts shedding or returning rented body parts. "Now both feet had returned to the owners, so he began to crawl along on the ground" (p. 20). Eventually he returns the belly, ribs and chest. After returning "the skin and flesh which covered the head" (p. 21), the complete gentleman is reduced to a skull. At the most obvious level it is xenophobia 101: the Complete Gentleman is the ultimate 'Other', embodying the unfamiliar, the monstrous and everything the community is not (Goodhead, 2018, pp. 69, 74).

But there is also a more constructive message that the complete gentleman conveys. He appears perfect, only to reveal that his extensions and body parts are all borrowed. Appearances are deceptive, and the human tendency to live by appearances, and activating oneself with technological extensions – the so-called jujus – is exposed. The beautiful lady wanted a man out of this world and that is what she got: an abstraction that does not exist. The Complete Gentleman is therefore always and already a work in progress. Tutuola thus adds another dimension to our understanding of intersectionality; he makes an explicit causal link between incompleteness and interdependence. It is not just a matter of multiple identities of gender, race, ethnicity, sexuality, class, etc. intersecting, but also recognition that all identities are never final; and because of that they require relations with other humans as well as non-humans (of conflict and/or cooperation/alliance) (Nyamnjoh, 2017, p. 2). Identity is often only sustained through relationships with incomplete 'Others' (Nyamnjoh, 2015a, pp. 1, 2). In this way, Tutuola confirms Afrocentric, but also specifically African, feminist principles of community and family (Kolawole, 2002).

If agency is also about humility in recognising one's own shortcomings and the need to rely on others, human and non-human (Nyamnjoh, 2017, pp. 5, 121), the liberal peacebuilding project is the complete antithesis. The Complete Gentleman represents the perfect package of post-conflict reconstruction initiatives, pre-packed by the international community as stabilisation first, disarmament, demobilisation and reintegration, peace negotiations and agreement, followed by the formation of an interim government, elections, security sector reform and other aspects of post-conflict recovery. Here we also have the delusion of Western, self-made individual perfection: insisting on models of state-building and peacebuilding that resemble their own flawed and incorrectly remembered experiences. But Tutuola tells us that imperfection or incompleteness necessitates interdependence and for that reason the Complete Gentleman, now reduced to Skull, must repay his debts, and cannot claim autonomy or boast about being self-made. If only the West could recognise the debt it owes others (Nyamnjoh, 2017, pp. 147, 149). Recognition of imperfect liberal peacebuilding would also be a step towards deeper local-global partnerships, with implications for gender and restorative justice, as well as how rule of law and impunity related to sexual and gender-based violence are approached.

Agency is not only complex and multi-faceted, but also fluid. In this regard, Tutuola illustrates the plastic quality of agency through the constant metamorphosis and intrinsic mutability of the drinkard. It means that questions of who is an African, or who belongs to what sex/gender cannot, be determined in advance. In this regard, Oyěwùmí (2006, pp. 256-259) challenges the Western binary construction of two biologic categories and contends that gender was not an organising principle in pre-colonial Yoruba society: it was a colonial construction. The fluidity of sex and gender categories in traditional Yoruba society speaks to Yoruba tolerance and embrace of ambiguity influenced by the Creole world of syncretism (Salamone, 2006, p. 211). Subtle indications of this gender fluidity appear in the form of the hero's wife giving birth through her thumb, a kind of outsourced pregnancy (Tutuola, 1952, p. 31; Nyamnjoh 2017, p. 192). There are many violent scenes in the book, perpetrated by genderless creatures or beings. Most of the time they are referred to in the plural, the so-called 'deads' or 'alives', or such and such creatures, etc. One of the few exceptions where gender is attached is in the case of the old woman, the Faithful-Mother, who lives in the White Tree and is painted as a benevolent figure, "only helping those who [are] in difficulties and enduring punishments but not killing anybody" (Tutuola, 1952, p. 67), reverting back to entrenched stereotypes. But on the whole, following Tutuola, any and every masculinity or femininity is never complete and in constant flux, as it interacts with others (Nyamnjoh 2017: 26).

A more modern-day application of gender fluidity in peacebuilding contexts could be the manifestation of shifting gender relations and gender behaviours during and after wars. Understanding these shifts better may hold the key to fostering long-term peace. Being able to adapt becomes an important coping strategy during and after war; for instance, when women's organisations exploit the availability of donor funding related to curbing sexual and gender-based violence by inflating victim statistics. Changing gender relations have proved to be a source of agency for many women in the Democratic Republic of Congo (DRC), who gained economic independence after the war. For men who lost their traditional role as warrior-protectors and breadwinners, it was a source of disempowerment. They suffered stigmatisation even more than women because they occupied a higher status in their communities. Changing gender relations can therefore become a source of tension, particularly when the changes come from within, from women/wives who are asserting their 'rights' at the expense of men 'who have become like women'. These examples show that agency is not an individualist act of free choice among various courses of action, in a world free from power asymmetries. Rather, agency comes from the intersected interaction between individuals, communities, societies and structures of domination (Western and non-Western). The way the individual at the everyday level navigates oppressive structures as forms of coping and survival strategies can lead to transformation (Hobson & Sajed, 2017, p. 549).

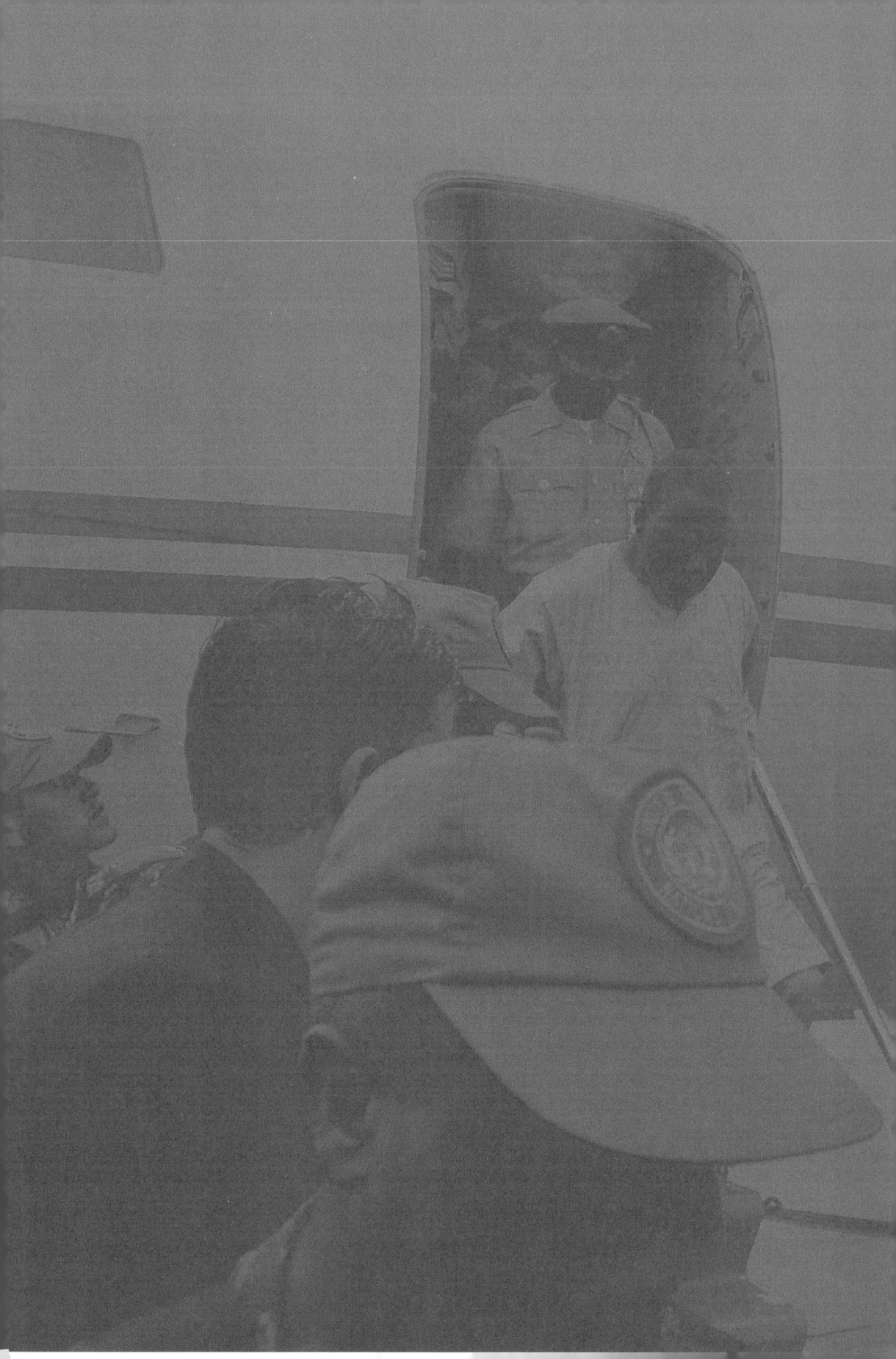

Roberts International Airport, Monrovia, Liberia, March 2006. Former Liberian President Charles Taylor alights from the Nigerian government plane into the waiting handcuffs of United Nations Peacekeepers. Photo: Mathew Elavanalthoduka, UN Photo.

"Can Tutuola offer a lens for understanding the power and leadership roles of these Big Men?

Shifting political identities: Big Men as complete gentlemen?

Change and identity shifts is also the theme of scholarly work on warlord democrats in Africa (Themnér, 2017). Can Tutuola offer a lens for understanding the power and leadership roles of these Big Men, the rebel leaders turned respectable politicians, the Jean-Pierre Bembas and Charles Taylors of Africa? Are they the proverbial complete gentlemen, who 'fake their way' through the difficult process of transforming themselves from wartime generals to post-war democrats or is the transformation genuine? How do they reconcile their many war and post-war identities?

The answers to these questions hinge on several factors; firstly, the tension between the formal and the informal. Institutions in these war-torn countries are weak; in fact, they are façades, fakes like the Complete Gentleman. And perhaps we can argue that stronger informal networks are actually the real systems. Yet, according to the international community, there is no alternative; it is the formal route or nothing:

> replac[ing] informal wartime governance structures – rebel groups, paramilitaries and black-market networks – with formal institutions – justice systems, legislatures, security forces and civil services – that are assumed to be more efficient, accountable and better at preventing renewed warfare (Themnér, 2017, pp. 7-8)

Secondly, empirical research on the possible links between the different types of masculinities that these Big Men embody would also tell us more about their gender identities. It would be wrong to assume that they only tick the 'hypermasculinity' box, and that their private and public identities are necessarily similar. For intersectionality to work, we need to see these Big Men, not for their ostensible agency and power, but for their 'half and half' identities, focusing on the hidden inequalities in their 'armour'. Thirdly, as Tutuola tells us, imperfection or incompleteness warrants interdependence, and the inevitability of networks of patronage. Networks come in different guises, through personalised power, but also through the gun. What jujus are they activating to gain support?

Ambivalent findings in terms of whether these Big Men are genuinely transforming from warlords to peacelords (see Themnér, 2017, p. 34: "chameleonic leadership") are significant because that confirms their hybrid status. Many contextual factors, such as electoral constraints, the nature of the patronage network, as well as non-text book socialisation into democracy, place the warlord democrats at the nexus between civil society and state. We cannot think of them as traditional Weberian actors (state, political party, civil society, armed forces, etc.). A Tutuolian lens helps us to look beyond the binary stereotype of either being "shepherds of peace" or "democratic spoilers" (p. 5) and underlines the need for nuanced views about leadership. Ultimately, as Tutuola shows us, power is derived from relationships with incomplete others. If we keep this in mind, it might be easier for the international community to work with rather than against the phenomenon of Big Incomplete Gentlemen in African politics.

I now turn to the second area where Tutuola extends feminist thinking on peace and security.

Niassa Province in Mozambique. Female war veterans who fought in the Mozambican war of independence from 1964 to 1974. Photo by Jonna Katto.

> **The everyday in peace-time or conflict is largely about bodily or sensory experience.**

Making the everyday spectral, spectacular and uncomfortable

One of the most significant contributions of feminist scholarship is the emphasis on the private, the informal, the local and the personal, and what it tells us about international and global structures. Enloe (2011, 2014), for instance, urges us to concern ourselves with "the seemingly unexceptional or inconsequential within global politics" (Jarvis, 2018, p. 8).

In peacebuilding terms, it means that we need to study the everyday practices and routines of diplomats, donors, NGO staff and military peacekeepers, as well as locals involved in peacebuilding. Part of such an endeavour is ethnographic in nature, but:

> It is not enough to know what is happening to men, women and children in war – and how those experiences differ – we should strive to know why, and how these various experiences are tied to political and economic structures, opportunities and incentives at local, national and international levels" (Mazurana & Proctor, 2013, p. 11)

In this regard, Jennings (2014) traces peacekeepers' interaction with locals in Liberia and the DRC. Her findings on the gendered and racialised nature of the day-to-day interactions – through domestic work, sex work and private security – reveal that locals often have more agency than expected.

The everyday in peacetime or conflict is largely about bodily or sensory experience: feeling, tasting, smelling, hearing and seeing the textures of war and peace (Sylvester, 2011). What makes these experiences significant is that they all remain the gendered and racialised experiences of ordinary people, not states. They are experienced first-hand, not through media, state discourse or filtered through a lens of academia. Specht's (2006) study of the experiences and motives of female ex-combatants in Liberia is illustrative. The research reveals multi-layered motives in girls taking up arms, such as purely economic need, linked to poverty, but also as a means of obtaining luxury items such as a pair of red shoes. A study of the life of a Liberian woman called 'Black Diamond', leader of the armed women's unit (Women's Artillery Commandos), a unit that fought with the rebel LURD (Liberians United for Reconciliation and Democracy), reveals how she was raped when she was 15 years old and forced to witness the killing of her parents. These experiences may have been productive in her becoming a leader her followers described as a fierce combatant yet kind to her troops (Holzner 2011). When humans interact with their material environment, these lived experiences form a 'meeting place' for intersected identities. Treating the everyday as a bona fide research site implies:

> taking the popular, the historical and the ethnographic seriously, and emphasizing interdependence and conviviality within and between different bodies of knowledge (disciplines) and between scholars, policy makers and practitioners (Nyamnjoh, 2017, p. 54)

It is this notion of the everyday as a meeting place between silos that makes it a site from where knowledge can be exchanged and challenged.

The everyday that we encounter in the underworld that the drinkard inhabits looks vastly different. Here *"reality is more than meets the eye and the world an experience of life beyond sensory perceptions"* (Nyamnjoh, 2017, p. 22, in italics in the original text). Tutuola presents worlds that are radically different from what is deemed 'normal' or 'natural'. Here you will find Death toiling in his own yam garden (p. 12)! Tutuola's everyday is marked by a mixture of the routine of eating, sleeping, etc. and a sense of anticipation and uncertainty driven by fear (of death) and pleasure, or what Nuttall (2001) describes as "hallucinatory qualities" (p. 397) of the spectral. With the power of fantasy also comes surprise (awe) and fear of a world of hidden knowledge contained in the non-human bodies of monsters, such as the red-fish, a monster to be conquered in order to free the community from the curse of annual human sacrifice (Tutuola, 1952, pp. 73-85), yet this monster "was laughing and coming towards me like a human-being, but I said within myself that this was a really human-being" (p. 80). The drinkard sells his death for 70 pounds (p. 67), and therefore cannot not die (p. 72), but keeps his fear. We have to bear the gruesome tale of how the drinkard burns the house down with his child inside, only for him to return as an even more vengeful Half-bodied Baby (pp. 34-35) who terrorises his parents, not allowing them to sleep or eat, and insisting on being carried around. This is a big monstrous child, with the power to change himself into something else (p. 31), described as a "wonderful" child (p. 33)! We witness the cruelty of the creatures in the Unreturnable-Heaven's Town: "unknown creatures, both adults and children…were looking for ways of making their cruelties [against humans] even worse; [they] held us firmly and the rest were beating us and also their children were stoning us repeatedly" (p. 58). The hero retaliates in self-defence, burning them and their children in their homes (p. 62). The Hungry-Creature swallows both the drinkard and his wife (p. 108); and the most terrible of all the deads are the Dead-Babies, who assault everyone they meet (p. 102).

It becomes an everyday of the imagination, where ordinary Africans are given the opportunity to become extraordinary. Spectral fantasy therefore does more than just mirror society; it transforms and points to an alternative imaginary for peacebuilding, that is at once utopian and dystopian, a good place and bad one; or as Kirby (2017) refers to it, "moving from *alterity* to *alternatives*" (p. 583, in italics in the original text). On the one hand, nature is humanised; for example, the White Tree has hands. On the other, humans have superhuman powers: the hero describes himself as the "Father of gods who could do everything in this world" (Tutuola, 1952, p. 10). By giving the non-human human form and consciousness and humans superhuman power, Tutuola collapses all the artificial boundaries between entrenched knowledges.

Feminist methodologies, such as the 'methodology of unease' developed by Baaz and Stern (2016) related to their work on sexual and gender-based violence in the DRC also make the strange familiar and the familiar strange. In their interviews with members of the armed forces (FARDC), Baaz and Stern (2016) used an intersectional lens to allow them to see soldiers not only as soldiers, but also as human beings, fathers, husbands and breadwinners. It allowed them to uncover alternative narratives about why men rape in war. Their field research revealed much ambivalence and many contradictions. The disjuncture between the soldiers' and women's narratives, and the researchers' preconceived notions of what they thought they knew before they entered the field, not only led to a sense of surprise (p. 126), but also to shame about their complicity in the maintenance of dominant hegemonic discourses about sexual violence. Their methodology of unease relied in part on teasing out how different understandings of gender inform the construction of different discourses of gender and sexual violence, locally and globally, as well as learning to deal with their emotions and affective responses. They also employed reflexivity and active listening, and recognised the epistemic role research subjects played in the research process. When subjects' personal experiences are taken seriously, they hold the potential to break through the abstract, universalised nature of Western research practices.

That said, the process of knowing described above remains largely within the confines of the body, heart and mind, and overlooks the spiritual dimension. The Afrocentric's attention to the spiritual is an area much neglected in Western social theory. The material world is contaminated by colonialism; the epistemological world also, but the spiritual – because it has been relegated to the hinterland or rather backyard – has to a large extent escaped the colonial influence and gaze, and is not dominated by the Western (see Shilliam in Hobson & Sajed, 2017, p. 549). The potential for theory-building by extracting knowledge from the spiritual world therefore offers huge possibilities for alternative imaginings.

Within Afrocentric methodologies there is an emphasis on the fact that not everything that matters is measurable. Intuition is considered a valid source of information. Nyamnjoh (2015a) accordingly reminds us that the "real is not only what is observable or what makes cognitive sense; it is also the invisible, the emotional, the sentimental, the intuitive and the inexplicable" (p. 37). In this world humans are decentred, though still important, but "[m]an has to struggle hard to ensure a place in the universe. He must compete with the rest of animated nature. He is no absolute monarch exerting untrammeled authority over the rest of the universe" (Obiechina, 1968, p. 88).

And it is here where Tutuola can assist us. He gives us a glimpse of a world that puts experience at a level beyond sensory perceptions. The drinkard and other characters in the book are able "to see, feel, hear, smell and taste things that are ordinarily beyond sight, feeling, hearing, smelling and tasting" (Nyamnjoh, 2015a, p. 9). It does not mean that we now have to call up spirits or speak to ancestors in order to have knowledge. What it does require is mindfulness not to simply and unreflectively insert the spiritual and unseen into Western understandings of peace. This will not dislodge the centre. The spiritual dimension also should not be equated with superstition, as this will reinforce old hierarchies. Fundamentally, the task at hand is a careful and informed recalibration, which will ask for critical reflections on how colonial conditions have shaped the field, thinking and practices of peacebuilding. As the story of the Complete Gentleman illustrates, we should not instinctively revert to sensory perceptions to label something or somebody as different; we must look deeper.

Detail from headdress for Efe of Gelede, Yoruba, Anago region, late 19th-early-mid-20th century. Gelede celebrates "Mothers" (awon iya wa), a group that includes female ancestors and deities as well as the elderly women of the community, and the power and spiritual capacity these women have in society. Photo: Art Institute of Chicago.

> **Women peacebuilders in Africa often go against Eurocentric notions of feminism, subversively using culture – and essence – to fight culture.**

Palm wine initiation vessel from Fontam, Bangwa, Cameroon grasslands. Photo: Ann Porteus.

From othering to liminality: implications for gender and peacebuilding

In tracking a possible way forward on how to use The Palm-Wine Drinkard as a lens for gender and peacebuilding practices, we need to consider the implications of space. Physical borders that divide sovereign territories play an important part in the story of The Palm-Wine Drinkard, and become representative of the practice of othering and the construction of difference, during colonial times as well as within the practice of peacebuilding. The idea of crossing a border is often associated with fear of trespassing. For instance, the Faithful-Mother stops short of the stream that separates her domain from the next territory (Tutuola, 1952, p. 71); the Mountain-Creatures could not cross the river (p. 117); and the Long White Creatures "were bound not to trespass on another's bush" (p. 43). The message is clear: certain areas are reserved for certain groups with specific physical appearances and essences, as are depicted in such cryptic labels as Sinners' Town, the Path of Death, the Town of the Multi-Coloured People, the Town Where Nobody Sings, the Red-People of the Red-Town, Deads' Town, Un-returnable-Heaven's Town (p. 57 ff), Wraith Island Town (p. 48), and beautiful people of the Faithful-Mother's hall (Krishnan, 2017, pp. 332-333). These are closed societies, not friendly towards foreigners. Or are they?

Paradoxically, while the boundaries appear to be fixed, the hero is able to cross them, although often with trepidation. So, maybe space is much more dynamic than we think. The colonial practice of separating populations that are actually deeply entangled has always been questionable. The fact that the drinkard is able to transcend spatial limitations makes him an ideal interlocutor. Wherever he goes, he has an impact on communities (Obiechina, 1968, p. 91), most of the time accidentally or out of self-defence, but still able to shift or revise the norms of that society (Krishnan, 2017, p. 335).

The palm-wine drinkard, as half-spirit and half-human, is therefore a liminal or hybrid life form, a composite figure able to collapse the boundaries between different worlds, of ghosts and of humans, representing the link between different sets of knowledges. Even when he changes himself into a canoe to ferry people over the river in order to earn money (Tutuola, 1952, p. 39) or into a bird (p. 40), fire (p. 42) or a self-propelled pebble (p. 117), he does not lose human consciousness and feels hungry (p. 45). It does not matter whether the container takes on human, non-human, animate, inanimate, visible or invisible form (Nyamnjoh, 2017, p. 28). It means that the body becomes a mere container or vessel for the enactment of multiple forms of consciousness, auras and essences (pp. 28, 138; Nyamnjoh, 2015a, p. 2). Tutuola therefore does more than just challenge the Cartesian mind/body dichotomy; his characters transcend it. They unite mind and body at the 'supra-natural' level of transcendental consciousness.

What can practitioners learn from the figure of the drinkard for their peacebuilding interventions? A combined and/or separate focus on one or all three of the following change areas could be a way to structure or frame an intervention:

- Change security institutions (institutional approach);
- Shift mindsets (a sociocultural approach) to foster peaceful masculinities and femininities; and
- Broaden inclusion through an intersectional approach to transform relations in the community and between peacebuilders and the community, taking a relational view of the dynamics in the community and the fact that problems should be solved not within a silo but from multiple perspectives (see Kuehnast & Robertson, 2018).

I reiterate that this is not a recipe, but rather a conceptual means of thinking differently about whose knowledge counts and how to make room for multiple local and international knowledges.

As a first possible 'step', peacebuilding practitioners need to draw on the feminist tools of intersectionality and the everyday, combined with Tutuola's notion of incompleteness, interdependence and the spectacular, and make it their business to understand how identity norms operate. The first 'action' therefore is one of cognition. Conflict is often the result of adherence to specific gender norms. Peacebuilders need to grasp that increasing militarisation of young men and widespread sexual violence affect everybody in that society, long after the war has ended (Kuehnast & Robertson, 2018, p. 2).

Both feminists and Tutuola ask that attention be paid to diverse experiences, asking who has control over resources and what the broader relationships and power dynamics across a society look like. For example, issues of reintegration affect different categories of women and men differentially, such as former women-combatants, bush wives not usually considered as combatants, women whose livelihoods was dependent on their involvement in the transfer of small arms, and male or female rape victims with or without HIV and AIDS. Practically, an intersectional lens enables the practitioner or policymaker to see who is the most vulnerable, whose attitudes pose a barrier, or whose attitudes and practices are most amenable to transformation (Myrttinen et al. 2014). The multiple intersecting identities of displaced persons affect the informal and formal roles that those men and women adopt. An intersectional approach based on incompleteness and interdependence can have benefits for budgeting as well. Understanding the complexity of identities will facilitate more specific targeting and increase the likelihood of money reaching the right group. The value of this approach lies in better understanding "how a person's multiple identities affect their influence and power in a given situation and thus to better understand how society may or may not be addressing their grievances" (Kuehnast & Robertson, 2018, p. 14).

As already mentioned in the previous section related to warlord democrats, it emphasises context. Such an approach helps to highlight the broader context of the conflict as well as the peace intervention. By ensuring that conflict analysis takes account of gender-relational power, better understanding is gained about the role of gender norms and behaviours in driving conflict and/or peace. Research shows that when civil society groups, including women's organisations are included in peace processes, the accords are 64 percent less likely to fail. Women tend to broaden the issues discussed beyond narrow military security concerns, thereby increasing the chances of addressing root causes of conflict and building much needed buy-in (Robertson & Thompson, 2018).

Tutuola's work, more so than feminist research, suggests that we need interlocutors to facilitate this process. A second possible step would be to identify change agents. Women and/or women's organisations in conflict and post-conflict situations are often seen as being close to the community, having access to intelligence where they act as bridge-builders between local and security policy communities. Their well-established and well-documented role in providing services to victims of rape or conflict resolution training further enhances their suitability as possible change agents. Women peacebuilders in Africa often go against Eurocentric notions of feminism, subversively using culture – and essence – to fight culture. For example, Women of Zimbabwe Arise, an organisation of men and women fighting for women's rights and broader political, social and economic justice in Zimbabwe demanded accountability from the government by using their role as mothers and homemakers to champion their cause, publicly protesting with brooms (the ultimate symbol of domestication), mimicking the sweeping away of corruption and bad governance (Mutisi, 2011, pp. 122-123). In Liberia, the Women in Peacebuilding Network, a women's peace group working across religious, ethnic and political lines, pressured the warlords and Liberian government to agree to peace through a rather unusual method: they took off their clothes in order to shame the men back to the negotiation table. The women drew on cultural taboos, as it is unacceptable for a man to see a mother or elderly woman naked. This act of defiance – the naked mother – simultaneously embodied vulnerability and agency (Holzner, 2011, p. 47).

As a last possible step, peacebuilders need to then facilitate connections and support intermediary figures in their change work. It is important to note in this regard that these interstitial figures need to be hybrid figures in the true sense of the word, and not elites in disguise. It is therefore not the kind of 'position' that everybody in the post-war situation will occupy. The interlocutors have to be committed to giving a voice to both the marginalised and those closer to formal power.

This would entail, firstly, raising uncomfortable questions about relations of (inter)dependence between 'us' (international peacebuilders) and 'them' (local peacebuilders, such as community leaders, chiefs, women's groups, etc.), each group with its own internal power relations as well. The issue of local ownership is hugely contested. Local-global partnerships are quite diverse and asymmetrical, with a disconnect between small-scale locally driven peacebuilding efforts and the large-scale external presence in conflict-prone states (Björkdahl & Höglund, 2013). Intervening actors brought in to stabilise the situation often ensconce themselves behind high walls and fortify their compounds, complete with lookout posts and high fences in the capitals of the states they work in. Such a retreat widens the distance between international and local actors, and raises questions about the kind of knowledge generated when these actors remove themselves from the very society they seek to help. Although many of these peacekeepers or private security personnel are often not Western soldiers, but rather Africans or from Asian states such as Pakistan and Bangladesh, their practices are explained by the fact that the African Union (AU) has bought into the liberal peacebuilding model. In spite of its rhetoric of inclusivity, and the development of a concept of post-conflict reconstruction and development, the AU foregrounds a liberal understanding of peacebuilding and the principle of gender equality as key to women's empowerment and broader peace and development on the continent.

Secondly, more emphasis should be placed on the fact that the formal is often dependent on the informal, both in terms of peacebuilding and security and the economy. Defying all boundaries in the way that feminist scholars and Tutuola do could work towards breaking down the artificial barriers between formal and informal peacebuilding, where women's role in informal peacebuilding is publicly celebrated, while they remain absent from formal peace negotiations. It could also contribute towards more attention being paid in the field of post-war economic recovery to how the formal economy is sustained by women's informal work. This understanding puts women's empowerment in an entirely different light. In the case of the example of the warlord democrats, there is also potential to view them differently; not as actors in the formal sphere of politics, but rather crossover actors with strong informal networks seeking to enter weak formal institutions. Lastly, there should be more awareness about knowledge creation as the result of complex interaction between multiple actors (i.e. academics, policymakers and practitioners).

Taken together in this context, the interlocutors become more than knowledge carriers and producers; they become cultural mediators capable of interrogating the global through the local, precisely because they inhabit in-between spaces not bound by nation states.

Amos Tutuolas's birth-town, Abeokuta, is the largest city and state capital of Ogun State in southwest Nigeria.
Photo: Melvin Baker, July 2006.

Conclusion

In sum, by making his characters 'shapeshifters', Tutuola allows humans to become gods/spirits and vice versa; and humans to transform themselves into spirits, animals and plants. At times, a creature combines multiple forms of being: half-human and half-animal or half-plant, half-god, etc. Agency is therefore infinite, fluid and dependent on context.

Tutuola's special brand of folklore is particularly insightful, because it not only enhances or reinforces feminist insights on gender binaries, but also pushes the boundaries of consciousness and extends feminist insights on the mind/body split. Creative merging of Afrocentric and feminist perspectives could potentially address the under-theorised and colonial character of peacebuilding in Africa. In peacebuilding terms, it means crafting a 'class' of peacebuilding analysts or practitioners who think more broadly about the whole of global politics as both human and gendered (and not just of women), as well as non-human (spiritual).

In conclusion, it might also be fitting to reflect on the role of peacebuilding scholars in particular. They could start with documenting multiple universes (ethnographically, literarily, historically, archeologically, etc.) for their epistemological significance. The process of documentation should focus on the manner in which these popular universes privilege consciousness over essence (Nyamnjoh, 2017, p. 274) and underscore the importance of relatedness, openness, not-knowing, humility and mutuality. Here, attention should be paid to intermediaries and their specific knowledge role; namely as narrators of a dynamic and fluid Africa that actively engages with global culture, but which is also able to generate its own authoritative representations in multiple locations of difference and transition. If this is done comparatively in relation to other continents and regions, it may very well contain the seeds of a more just and inclusive process of knowledge and theory-building. In this way we can also circumvent the trap of exceptionalising Africa by mistaking the spiritual for superstition.

Bibliography

Arowosegbe, J. O. (2012). The Making of an Organic Intellectual: Claude Ake, Biographical and Theoretical Orientations. African and Asian Studies, 11, 123-143.

Baaz, M. E., & Stern, M. (2013). Sexual Violence as a Weapon of War? Perceptions, Prescriptions, Problems in the Congo and Beyond. New York: Zed.

Bercovitch, J., & Jackson, R. (2009). Conflict resolution in the twenty-first century. Principles, methods, and approaches. Ann Arbor: University of Michigan Press.

Björkdahl, A., & Höglund, K. (2013). Precarious peacebuilding: friction in global-local encounters. Peacebuilding, 1(3), 289-299.

Cockburn, C. (2007). From where we stand. War, women's activism and feminist analysis. London: Zed.

Crenshaw, K. (1991). Mapping the margins: Intersectionality, identity politics and violence against women of color. Stanford Law Review, 43(6), 1241-1299.

Duffield, M. (2001). Global Governance and the New Wars: The Merging of Development and Security. London: Zed.

Edkins, J. (2013). Novel writing in international relations: Openings for a creative practice. Security Dialogue, 44(4), 281-297.

Enloe, C. (2011). The Mundane Matters. International Political Sociology, 5(4), 447-450.

Enloe, C. (2014). Bananas, Beachers and Bases: Making Feminist Sense of International Politics. Berkeley: University of California Press.

Florence, N. (2013). Bukusu (Kenya) Folktales. International Feminist Journal of Politics, 15(3), 370-390.

Goodhead, D. (2018). Tradition and the African Children's Storyteller: The Example of Amos Tutuola and Ama Ata Aidoo. Folklore, 129(1), 58-77.

Hart, C. (2009). In search of African literary aesthetics: Production and reception of the texts of Amos Tutuola and Yvonne Vera. Journal of African Cultural Studies, 21(2), 177-195.

Hobson, J. M., & Sajed, A. (2017). Navigating Beyond the Eurofetishist Frontier of Critical IR Theory: Exploring the Complex Landscapes of Non-Western Agency. International Studies Review, 19(4), 547-572.

Holzner, B. M. (2011). War, bodies, and development. In C. Sylvester (Ed.), Experiencing War, pp. 42-63. London & New York: Routledge.

Jarvis, L. (2018). Toward a Vernacular Security Studies: Origins, Interlocutors, Contributions, and Challenges. International Studies Review, April, 1-20, https://doi.org/10.1093/isr/viy017.

Jennings, K. M. (2014). Service, sex, and security: Gendered peacekeeping economies in Liberia and the Democratic Republic of the Congo. Security Dialogue, 45(4), 313-330.

Keet, A. (2018, July 23). The Plastic University. Knowledge, Disciplines and Decolonial 'Circulations'. Inaugural Lecture. North Campus of Nelson Mandela University, South Africa. Retrieved from https://www.academia.edu/37278671/Draft_-_The_Plastic_University_-_Knowledge_Disciplines_and_Decolonial_Circulations

Kirby, P. (2017). Political Speech in Fantastical Worlds. International Studies Review, 19(4), 573-596.

Kolawole, M. M. (2002). Transcending Incongruities: Rethinking Feminism and the Dynamics of Identity in Africa. Agenda, 54, 92-98.

Krishnan, M. (2017). From Empire to Independence: Colonial Space in the Writing of Tutuola, Ekwensi, Beti, and Kane. Comparative Literature Studies, 54(2), 329-357.

Kuehnast, K., & Robertson, D. (2018). Gender Inclusive Framework and theory. A Guide for turning Theory into Practice. Washington, DC United States Institute of Peace. Retrieved from https://www.usip.org/sites/default/files/2018-08/gender-inclusive-framework-and-theory-guide.pdf.

Long, W. (2016, October 9). Op-Ed: The recolonising danger of decolonising psychology. Daily Maverick. Retrieved from http://www.dailymaverick.co.za/article/2016-10-09-op-ed-the-recolonising-danger-of-decolonising-psychology/#.WBb1zRtf3cs.

Lugones, M. (2008). The Coloniality of Gender. Worlds & Knowledges Otherwise, 2, Dossier 2, Spring, 1-17.

Lugones, M. (2010). Toward a Decolonial Feminism. Hypatia, 25(4), 742-759.

Mama, A. (1995). Beyond the Masks: Race, Gender and Subjectivity. New York: Routledge.

Mazurana, D., & Proctor, K. (2013, October 15). Gender, Conflict and Peace. Occasional Paper. World Peace Foundation. Retrieved from https://sites.tufts.edu/wpf/files/2017/04/Gender-Conflict-and-Peace.pdf.

Moore, G. (1975). Amos Tutuola: A Nigerian Visionary. In ed. B. Lindfors (Ed.), Critical Perspectives on Amos Tutuola (pp. 49-57). Washington, D.C.: Three Continents Press.

Mutisi, M. (2011). Countering the Currents: Zimbabwe. In S. I. Cheldelin & M. Eliamtamby (Eds.), Women Waging War and Peace. International Perspectives of Women's Role in Conflict and Post-Conflict Reconstruction (pp. 117-138). New York: Continuum.

Myrttinen, H., Naujoks, J., & El-Bushra, J. (2014). Rethinking Gender in Peacebuilding. International Alert. Retrieved from http://www.internationalalert.org/sites/default/files/Gender_RethinkingGenderPeacebuilding_EN_2014.pdf.

Nuttall, S. (2001). Reading, Recognition and the Postcolonial. Interventions, 3(3), 391-404.

Nyamnjoh, F. B. (2015a). Amos Tutuola and the Elusiveness of Completeness. Stichproben. Wiener Zeitschrift für kritische Afrikastudien, 15(29), 1-47.

Nyamnjoh, F. B. (2015b). Incompleteness. Frontier Africa and the Currency of Conviviality. Journal of Asian and African Studies, 52(3), 253-270.

Nyamnjoh, F. B. (2017). Drinking from the Cosmic Gourd. How Amos Tutuola Can Change Our Minds. Mankon, Bamenda: Langaa Research & Publishing CIG.

Obiechina, E. N. (1968). Amos Tutuola and the Oral Tradition. Présence Africaine, 65, 85 106.

Omelsky, M. (2018). The Creaturely Modernism of Amos Tutuola. Cultural Critique, 99, 66 96.

Oyěwùmí, O. (2006). Colonizing Bodies and Minds. From: The Invention of Women: Making an African Sense of Western Gender Discourse. Minneapolis: University of Minnesota Press. In B. Ashcroft, G. Griffiths & H. Tiffin (Eds.), The Post-Colonial Studies Reader (2nd ed., pp. 256-259). London & New York: Routledge.

Paris, R., & Sisk, T. (Eds.). (2009). The dilemmas of statebuilding. Confronting the contradictions of postwar peace operations. London: Routledge.

Petra Peacebuilders. 2018. What is a Peacebuilder? Retrieved from http://www.petra-peacebuilders.org/who-is-a-peacebuilder/.

Pratt, N., & Richter-Devroe, S. (2011). Critically examining UNSCR 1325 on Women, Peace and Security. International Feminist Journal of Politics 13(4), 489-503.

Robertson, D. & Thompson, T. (2018, October 18). If we want to build peace, we can't keep women out. Analysis and Commentary. United States Institute of Peace. Retrieved from https://www.usip.org/publications/2018/10/if-we-want-build-peace-we-cant-keep-women-out

Rojas, C. (2016). Contesting the Colonial Logics of the International: Toward a Relational Politics for the Pluriverse. International Political Sociology, 10(4), 369-382.

Salamone, F. (2006). The Depiction of Masculinity in Classic Nigerian Literature. Journal of the African Literature Association, 1(1), 202-213.

Specht, I., & Crisis Response and Reconstruction. (2006). Red shoes: experiences of girl-combatants in Liberia. International Labour Organization.

Sylvester, C. (2011). Experiencing War. London & New York: Routledge.

Themnér, A. (2017). Introduction – Warlord democrats: wartime investments, democratic returns? In A. Themnér (Ed.), Warlord democrats in Africa. Ex-military leaders and electoral politics (pp. 1-40). London: Zed.

Tobias, S. M. (1999). Amos Tutuola and the Colonial Carnival. Research in African Literatures, 30(2), 66-74.

Tucker, K. (2018). Unraveling Coloniality in International Relations: Knowledge, Relationality, and Strategies for Engagement. International Political Sociology 12, 215-232.

Tutuola, A. (1952). The Palm-Wine Drinkard and his Dead Palm-Wine Tapster in the Deads' Town. London: Faber and Faber.

VanderMeer, J. (2013, January 7) Amos Tutuola. An interview with Yinka Tutuola. Weird Fiction Review. Retrieved from http://weirdfictionreview.com/2013/01/amos-tutuola-an-interview-with-yinka-tutuola-by-jeff-vandermeer/

About the Claude Ake Visiting Chair and Memorial Paper

The Claude Ake Visiting Chair was set up in 2003 by the Department of Peace and Conflict Research, Uppsala University (DPCR) and the Nordic Africa Institute (NAI) with funding from the Swedish government and Uppsala University. The chair honours the memory of Professor Claude Ake, a distinguished scholar, philosopher, teacher and humanist, who died tragically in 1996. The chair is intended for scholars who, like Claude Ake, combine a profound commitment to scholarship with a strong advocacy for social justice. It is open to social scientists working at African universities with research on war, peace, conflict resolution, human rights, democracy and development on the African continent. The visiting chair holder is offered a conducive environment to pursue his or her own research.

Based on the research project that they pursue while in Uppsala, the holders of the Claude Ake Visiting Chair give a public lecture. The topic of the lecture shall, in a general sense, relate to the work of Claude Ake, for example in terms of themes or issues covered, or in the theoretical or normative points of departure. The lecture is based on a paper prepared and made available to seminar participants and lecture audience in advance of the lecture. The paper is subsequently published jointly by DPCR and NAI in the Claude Ake Memorial Paper (CAMP) series. Below is a list of previous titles in the series:

1. JINADU, L. Adele; Explaining and Managing Ethnic Conflict in Africa: Towards a Cultural Theory of Democracy (2007)

2. OBI, Cyril I.; No Choice, But Democracy: Prising the People out of Politics in Africa? (2008)

3. SESAY, Amadu; The African Union: Forward March or About Face-Turn? (2008)

4. BOAFO-ARTHUR, Kwame; Democracy and Stability in West Africa: The Ghanaian Experience (2008)

5. VILLA-VICENCIO, Charles; Where the Old Meets the New: Transitional Justice, Peacebuilding and Traditional Reconciliation Practices in Africa (2009)

6. MOHAMED, Adam Azzain; Evaluating the Darfur Peace Agreement: A Call for an Alternative Approach to Crisis Management (2009)

7. MBABAZI, Pamela K; The Oil Industry in Uganda: A Blessing in Disguise or an all Too Familiar Curse? (2013)

8. ADETULA, Victor A.O.; African Conflicts, Development and Regional Organisations in the Post-Cold War International System (2015)

9. GOBODO-MADIKIZELA, Pumla; What Does It Mean to be Human in the Aftermath of Historical Trauma? Re-envisioning The Sunflower and Why Hannah Arendt was Wrong (2016)

10. MURITHI, Tim; Regional Reconciliation in Africa: The Elusive Dimension of Peace and Security (2019)

All titles can be downloaded in full text for open access. Please visit NAI's online research publication database DiVA at http://nai.diva-portal.org.

Lightning Source UK Ltd.
Milton Keynes UK
UKHW052241040319
338469UK00006B/130/P